P   L   A   C   E   D

K A R E S A N S U I   P O E M S

Counterpath Press
Denver, Colorado
www.counterpathpress.org

Printed in the United States of America

Library of Congress Cataloging-in-Publication Data

Snow, Carol, 1949–
     Karesansui poems / Carol Snow.
          p.   cm.
     ISBN 978-1-933996-09-7 (pbk. : alk. paper)
     I. Title.
PS3569.N57K37   2008
811'.54—dc22

                                        2008030070

Distributed by Small Press Distribution
(www.spdbooks.org)

PLACED

Carol Snow

COUNTERPATH PRESS

DENVER, COLORADO

2008

CONTENTS

The [Muramachi] era finds its garden prototype in
the scenery of the *kare-sansui*, the small-scale dry
landscape garden attached to and bordered by Shoin-
style architecture. Such gardens are designed to be
contemplated, like a painting, from a number of fixed
vantage points.

—Günter Nitschke, *Japanese Gardens:*
Right Angle and Natural Form

aboard about above across after against along amid
amidst among amongst around at athwart before behind
below beneath beside besides between betwixt beyond
but by concerning considering despite down during
ere except excepting for from in inside into like near
notwithstanding of off on outside over past pending
regarding respecting round save saving since through
throughout till to toward towards under underneath
unlike until unto up upon with within without

—The Seventy Prepositions, according to
Mrs. Lenore Larney, Aptos Junior High School
ca. 1962

. . .

I do survive beside the garden I

came seven thousand mile the other way
supplied all of engines to see, to see.
Differ them photographs, plans lie:
how big it is!
austere a sea rectangular   of sand by the oiled mud wall,
and the sand is not quite white: granite sand, grey,

—from nowhere can one see *all* the stones—

—John Berryman, from "Dream Song 73:
Karesansui, Ryoan-ji"

PLACED

In the subtexts, numbers refer to line number; unattributed poems are by the author.

"an ancient pond—
frog jumps in,
the sound of water"

KARESANSUI

"an ancient pond" — lexicon — "with the thought /
phrase" — "As Syllable from" — "chosen and placed"

Epigraph) Matsuo Bashō   1) Bashō; "Trace"   2) "Trace," continued;
Emily Dickinson, "[The Brain – is wider than the Sky –]"; "For"

"I was surprised, as I left the Museum, by the variety
of individual smiles on each of these mask-like
countenances [in a hundred studies for portraits by
Quentin-Latout];
though natural and charming on the whole, they had
made such an impression on me that my own face
was aching as if I had been smiling for hours."

1, 2) Henri Matisse, "Portraits", in Jack Flam, *Matisse on Art*

ABOUT

what one cannot face — "gets a look at those feet" —
   in extremis — back —
defining . . . — "tuning fork, metronome" —
   . . . defining — "and rushes back"

1) Professor Wagstaff (Groucho Marx) explains blood circulation in
Horse Feathers   2) "Koan/Coined"; Wagstaff, continued

ABOVE

"but helicopters or   a Brooklyn reproduction
  will fix that —"

"I was faced by the trouble that I" — "Differ them
    photographs," — "had acquired all this knowledge"
    — "plans lie:" — "gradually
but" — "how big it is!" — "when I had it" —
    " . . . —from nowhere" — "I had it" — "can one
    see" — "completely" — "*all*" — "at one time." —
    "the stones—"

Epigraph) John Berryman, "Dream Song 73: *Karesansui, Ryoan-ji*"
1) Gertrude Stein, "The Gradual Making of The Making of
Americans"; Berryman; Stein; Berryman; Stein   2) Stein,
continued; Berryman; Stein; Berryman; Stein; Berryman; Stein;
Berryman; Stein; Berryman

ACROSS

each of its stones its own — on the scale of — : from
  me —
a distance: an ocean

"That it should come to this" — "fifteen changeless
    stones in their five worlds / . . . of the ancient maker
    priest" — as Rembrandt [showed us he]
knew he'd become paint — that it should

1) William Shakespeare, *Hamlet,* act 1, scene 2; John Berryman,
"Dream Song 73: *Karesansui, Ryoan-ji*"

AGAINST

wouldn't just anyone stiffen? — pressed — what must
   be a muzzle — instead of no — no

"In the constantly moving stream of money" . . . of
     displaced attention — "the stones, as described
     above," — "vacancies bloom around extinct lives":
     hollows surround the impediments — "Identi-kit
(or *l'identi-kit,* as the French foppishly call it)" —
     in the _____ we call home — "were often
     deliberately selected and assembled"

1) Joshua Clover, "Chreia"; Irmtraud Schaarschmidt-Richter and
Osamu Mori, *Japanese Gardens,* introduction; Michele Glazer,
"And Sand Dollars"; Peter Cook and Alan Bennett, "The Great
Train Robbery," *Beyond the Fringe* 2) Cook and Bennett,
continued ("*l'identikit*" pronounced as in French: *lee-dahn-ti-kee'*);
Schaarschmidt-Richter and Mori, continued

AMID

"the sound of water"

"a sea rectangular" — "the way the drowned leave
    their names" — "a woman / thinks she belongs
    in a bathtub" — obsessing: if I have to think I
    am writing about it to pay attention — "in, / the
    sound" . . . *splash,*
splash! then birdsong (there, Ryoan-ji; here, a
    mockingbird)

Epigraph) Matsuo Bashō, "an ancient pond"   1) John Berryman,
"Dream Song 73: *Karesansui, Ryoan-ji*"; Laura Mullen, "Sestina
in Which My Grandmother Is Going Deaf"; "Living in Venice";
Bashō

"The original body remains clear constantly."

"To put it a little differently: one reason why the idea
of designing a garden with groups of rocks could be
adopted so swiftly and realized so splendidly from
early times, as we can see from early picture scrolls
and some actual surviving examples, may have been
that there was at least a specific attitude to the rock.
An aesthetic element is almost always inherent in
a religious connection, which meant that formal
qualities were recognized and seen, as well as the
numinous. This hypothesis is supported by the
fact that the stones, as described above, were often
deliberately selected and assembled."

"Speech and words cannot hinder it."

Epigraph) Zen Master Seung Sahn after Pai Chang, "Just-Like-This
Is Buddha," 1) Irmtraud Schaarschmidt-Richter and Osamu Mori,
Japanese Gardens, introduction   Epigraph) Seung Sahn, continued

AMONG

the way — from here to Ryoan-ji: contiguous

~ ~ ~

leaning over the oysterbed, he looked — classic —
    choosing among the existing —
"Crochet, souls, philosophy . . . " — approving/
    murderous — moving about

AMONGST

2) Fernando Pessoa, "Impassively"

AROUND

"Winter seclusion—
once more I will lean
against this post"

at the head of their stairs, a winged, torch-bearing
    cherub ("Jeanette, Isabella") wall sconce
    whimsically ceiling-mounted — "what is past, or
    passing, or to come" — banked — "Here we go
    'round" — backward, forward
crossovers — planetary — "once more I will lean / "

Epigraph) Matsuo Bashō 1) "Bring a Torch, Jeanette, Isabella,"
old French Christmas carol; William Butler Yeats, "Sailing to
Byzantium"; " . . . the mulberry bush" 2) "crossovers," viz., in
figure skating; Bashō

AT

"*Watching the goldfish* // (why?)" — "as tugged" —
      'caught my' — "—from nowhere can one see *all* the
      stones—" — "I love that cabbage butterfly
as if it were a fluttering corner of truth itself!" — And
      what about zombies? They stare straight ahead.

1) "By the Pond"; "Bowl"; John Berryman, "Dream Song 73:
Karesansui, Ryoan-ji"; Tomas Tranströmer, "Streets in Shanghai"
2) Tranströmer, continued

~ ~ ~

sweeping — "driven into desperate terms" — sponging
   one corner of the floor, May his heart be cleansed
   (3/20/2003) — *behind closed doors* — "The Lady, or
   the Tiger?" —

ATHWART

"The Lady, or the Tiger, or the Closet?" — "When
   Yantou came to Deshan, he straddled the threshold
   of the gate and asked, 'Ordinary, or holy?'" —
   "—and the news / Is war" — driven to symbolism
   — neither here nor there

1) William Shakespeare, *Hamlet*, act 4, scene 3; Frank R. Stockton
story title   2) Roz Chast cartoon caption; Thomas Cleary, *Book
of Serenity*, "Case [Koan] 22: Yantou's 'Bow and Shout'"; George
Oppen, "Of Being Numerous": "—and the news / Is war // As
always / That the juices may flow in them / Tho the juices lie."

intro arpeggio, arpeggio—cheers, applause—end
    intro, now sweet James sings the first line
of "Fire and Rain"—more whistles and cheers—the
    cognoscenti, then the fans: *I want to hear this* —
    "akin to the 'dawning' of . . . / joy on the face of an
    approached, recognizing" — it has already started

1) James Taylor, *Best Live* 2) "Conversion ('Spin')"

BEHIND

we couldn't help ourselves — *Crack!* (foul ball) and a
    swell in the sea of fans behind third base — cloud
    chamber:
tracings — "Everything stated or expressed by man is a
    note in the margin of a completely erased text." —
    and effect

's effect

2) Fernando Pessoa, "Peristyle"

BELOW

mantra — "beneath," the word "beneath": under the
    breath — 'deeper' reality? — as if to say — near —
    "The heaven
we are not allowed to see in this life: Om" — "Nearer,
    my"

    "God moves in a long *o*."

1) Joshua Clover, "Union pacific"   2) Clover, continued; Sarah
Adams lyric, "Nearer, My God, to Thee"   Epigraph) Dylan
Thomas, source unknown

particularly appreciative of the relatively flat: an
    expanse of water, ice rink, "dry-landscape garden
    (*karesansui*) with stone arrangement in seven-five-
    three rhythm (*shichigosan*) on white sand" — *once
    burned, twice shy* —
from childhood? — as for towering peaks: forget it

1) Irmstraud Schaarschmidt-Richter and Osamu Mori, *Japanese
Gardens*, caption to plate 17, Ryōanji Temple, Kyōto

"Or madly squeeze a right-hand foot
Into a left-hand shoe"

BESIDE

"Compare and contrast." — sorrow of — insistent —
    beside —
kindness — it had been forever

Epigraph) Lewis Carroll, "A-sitting On A Gate," *Through the Looking-Glass,* chapter 8   1) Maurice F. Englander, English exams, Lowell High School

"speech and words" — notes on the subject —
    "Against a ground of real wallpaper, Picasso sets
    a real newspaper clipping, a piece of sheet music,
    a charcoal drawing of a 'Cubist' wine glass, and
    four pieces of cut paper that evoke rather than
    directly" — "The name of the jeweler stands over
    the shop door in large *inlaid* letters—inlaid with
    fine imitation gems." — as if to say — "gray light
    streaking each bare branch, / each single twig,
    along one side, /
making another tree, of glassy veins . . . " — "We do
    not so much *see* the guitar in this picture as sense
    that it is being *named*."

1) Zen Master Seung Sahn after Pai Chang, "Just-Like-This Is
Buddha"; Jack Flam (on Picasso's *Guitar, Sheet Music and Glass*,
1912), *Matisse and Picasso*, chapter 6; Eduard Kroloff, *Schilderungen
aus Paris*, quoted by Walter Benjamin, "A [Arcades, Magasins de
Noveautiés, Sales Clerks]"; Elizabeth Bishop, "Five Flights Up"
2) Bishop, continued; Flam

BETWEEN

repositioned on the loop — Self and Other — -reliant
  — I foreswore (as companions)
objets — inert: *nature morte* — since our eyes met

BETWIXT

something in time — like a phrase — synapsed —
   between us — valenced — something in-
between us

BEYOND

" . . . *v' yeesh'tabach, v' yeetpa'ar, v' yeetrohmam, v'
yeet'nasei, v' yeet'hadar, v' yeet'aleh . . .* "

"She neither hears nor sees;
Rolled round in earth's diurnal course,
  With rocks, and stones, and trees."

"and tomorrow" — "And yet, and yet—" — "And
  death shall have no" — "to Mal Waldron and
  everyone
and I" — "a long / wonder the world can bear & be"
  — "*v' yeetkadash*" ["and sanctified"]: consoled by
  the *vs's* of the Kaddish

Epigraph) Mourners' Kaddish, traditional Jewish prayer
(" . . . praised, glorified, exalted, extolled, mighty, upraised, [and
lauded be the Name of the Holy One, Blessed is He]"); William
Wordsworth, "A Slumber Did My Spirit Seal" 1) William
Shakespeare, *Macbeth*, act 5, scene 5; Kobayashi Issa, "[The world
of dew]"; Dylan Thomas, "And Death Shall Have No Dominion";
Frank O'Hara, "The Day Lady Died" 2) O'Hara, continued; John
Berryman, "Dream Song 1"; Kaddish

BUT

built a skeleton of twigs — in such as this —
    constellation — animation technique: electrodes/
    sensors
strategically placed on the face, body — * * * — 'of
    the matter'

BY

"Fig. 2. A depiction of 'craggy mountains with gnarled trees,' here the setting for a hermit's hut. From the *Mustard Seed Garden Manual of Painting*, a sourcebook of Chinese painting techniques."

cutting, bulimia . . . — "'It's my own invention — '" — *constellation of symptoms*

Epigraph) David A. Slawson, *Secret Teachings in the Art of Japanese Gardens*, chapter 1 1) Lewis Carroll, *Through the Looking-Glass*, chapter 8

CONCERNING

"Absolute attention is prayer." Swell. Vocation without
    any leverage — but please — on tenterhooks, at
    gunpoint, pre-CAT scan — *out of the frying pan* —
    things go . . . — not 'and,' not yet

1) Simone Weil, source unknown

"A coward dies a thousand deaths, the hero dies but one."

CONSIDERING

some act/experience resists description — *beggaring*
    — "a coward . . . a thousand" — that which
    demanded a
threshold language — said of it: something held me
    back

Epigraph) "Cowards die many times before their deaths; / The
valiant never taste of death but once," William Shakespeare, *Julius
Caesar,* act 2, scene 2

DESPITE

"Futile – the Winds –
To a Heart in port – "

besieged — the protocol — "sets forth the 'Great
    Doctrine'" — "you must go on," — each stone,
    aura'd, continually assertive — extending — "*Her*
    chart
read Good, Very Good, Extreme Good—and Bitter
    Good." — "I can't go on, I'll go on" — intending:
    against

Epigraph) Emily Dickinson, ["Wild Nights – Wild Nights!"]
1) Eugen Herrigel, *Zen in the Art of Archery*; Samuel Beckett, *The Unnamable*; Clara Claiborne Park, *Exiting Nirvana*, chapter 5
2) Park, continued; Beckett

"The 'quantum jump' visualized as a sort of ladder."

DOWN

a passage — "notes in the margin" — on the scale of
   — "contemplation must be put on trial" —
   . . . *for your thoughts* — a century of pleasures, of
   particles,
of clouds — Project — a penny arcade

Epigraph) James Gleick, *Genius* 1) Fernando Pessoa, "Peristyle";
Walter Benjamin, "First Sketches," *The Arcades Project*: "In *The
Arcades Project*, contemplation must be put on trial. But it should
defend itself brilliantly and justify itself."

DURING

P for Procedure — came to mind most of, "the longest,
    hardest burning of that secret place" — in lieu of —
    easier said than — language,
sedative language — while it lasted

1) LEEP: loop electrosurgical excision procedure; Joanna Greenburg
(as Hannah Green), *I Never Promised You a Rose Garden,* chapter 6

streets of the known city — pre-emptive nostalgia —
    Camelot — moving water
in the known harbor — "Suddenly, unlike Bach":
    at least there's . . . the Laws of Nature . . . "what
    persists" . . . "whichever one is eternal—" . . . "a
    little of what persists and all the rest" . . . at least,
    will have been

2) John Berryman, "Henry's Confession"; Robert Hass, "Not Going
to New York: A Letter"; Brenda Hillman, "Time Problem"; Jorie
Graham, "To the Reader"

EXCEPT

"Nothing is either good or bad," — the policies: the
    casualties — "Just this
is it." — "but thinking makes it"

1) William Shakespeare, *Hamlet*, act 5, scene 3; Zen Master Yunyan
in Thomas Cleary, *Book of Serenity*, "Case 49: Dongshan Presents
Offerings Before the Image" 2) Yunyan, continued; Shakespeare

EXCEPTING

    "There can be a brick
    In a brick wall
    The eye picks"

"Nothing is either good or bad, but thinking makes"
    — "of truth itself" — "one corner" . . . "this
    small corner" — beside — "Elsewhere occurs—I
    remembers—
loss" — just — "The eye picks // So quiet of a Sunday"
    — " . . . so."

Epigraph) George Oppen, "Of Being Numerous" 1) William
Shakespeare, *Hamlet*, act 5, scene 3; Tomas Tranströmer, "Streets of
Shanghai"; "Athwart"; "Saving"; John Berryman, "Dream Song 73:
Karesansui, Ryoan-ji" 2) Berryman, continued; Oppen; Shakespeare

"Fig. 22. *Daitoku-ji* garden. This exemplifies the technique of borrowed scenery: the outside mountain on the left is incorporated into the design and is seen through the trees from inside the garden."

FOR

Epigraph) Kazuhiko Fukuda, *Japanese Stone Gardens*

on the scale of — a painting: a postcard — passage —
    Matisse. *The Piano Lesson* — "as tugged" . . . "as
    toward prey" . . . "defining . . . defining" — his son
    at the keyboard; in place of one eye,
an echo of the shape of the metronome

1) "Bowl"; "Bridge"; "About"

IN

the stones: their qualities in relation — *o* — I mean to
　say — occurs;
like shock, occurs — is located

INSIDE

rose an image — "—in what box?—" — tongue in
    the mouth, organs in the bodily frame — Dear
    Diary, — vowels between consonants — polar bear
    munching
on a cartoon igloo: "I just love these things! . . .
    Crunchy on the outside . . . " — the verb "is" in a
    sentence

1) "Bit"   2) Gary Larson cartoon caption: "Oh hey! I just love these
things! . . . Crunchy on the outside and a chewy center!"

INTO

"the longest, hardest burning of that secret place"

phrase — stepped onto the playing field — "This
    David was a giant and represented the decision to
    enter the battle" . . . "Day by day I found myself
    slipping more easily into the ceremony which sets
    forth the 'Great Doctrine' of archery" — the way
    — from "the"
(legato, a musical phrase: from "a" to "phrase") to
    "place"

Epigraph) Joanne Greenberg (as Hannah Green), *I Never Promised
You a Rose Garden,* chapter 6   1) Note: "onto" was not included in
Mrs. Larney's list of seventy prepostions; Eugen Herrigel, *Zen in the
Art of Archery*

LIKE

two ice cream flavors: a chocolate mint chip he
    described as "the staff of life," White Russian
    (kahlua vanilla)
she said was mother's milk to her

1) Double Rainbow brand; Ben & Jerry's brand

at the root of listening — *hmmm* — not descriptive —
waves —
near — "privilege of" — came in waves

2) Jane Austen, *Pride and Prejudice*, chapter 31

NOTWITHSTANDING

"*Amor fati* / The love of fate" — but *uh-oh* — will
    never know whether it would have been better to —
    missing —
so when the artist extends his thumb before the
    subject: what's that about? — what (could have)
    happened? — still missing — happened

1) George Oppen, "Of Being Numerous"

"I: Hints need the widest sphere in which to swing . . .
J: . . . where mortals go to and fro only slowly."

our — swing set swing — Ur of — invented perfecting

Epigraph) Martin Heidegger, "A Dialog on Language"

OFF

the slippage — names, especially — Chinese/Sanskrit
    terms for forms and poses
and their relation to Babel: "Yes, teacher" — *shrug* —
    "Shoo, fly" — "Nice to meet you."

2) "Shoo Fly, Don't Bother Me," traditional folk song

~ ~ ~

buoys marked the crab traps — directly upon reading
    "Handwriting Analysis" (Mom's *Big Book of Fun*:
    raveling, water-stained red cover, yellowing pages),
    my adopting the Greek ∂ ("creativity") — parterre,
    its gravel
raked into strokes — impasto: nymphéas — spared the
    depths, the focusing-into — *v[ersus]* the hook of
    the *y*

ON

of oneself — "∂" — "How little is still enough?" —
    seized upon — see:
Picasso. *Guitar, Sheet Music and Glass ("La Bataille
    s'est engagé[e]")* — not in sleep — the materials —
    outside [of]

1) "On"; Indigo Som, artist's statement, 2003 2) Pablo Picasso, late
1912: pasted papers, gouache and charcoal on paper, 48 x 36.5 cm;
"the materials" after George Oppen

should you want to return here — "preserved the ticket
   — the very" — litany — reread (in what tense?)
   "reread" — at/
present — Period. — "What is a sentence."

   "What is a sentence. They sent preserves."

1) "To" 2, Epigraph) Gertrude Stein, "Sentences"

PAST

the — post- — after: "the readiness is all"

1) William Shakespeare, *Hamlet,* act 5, scene 2

.

PENDING

on — addiction — haunting, 'catchy' — shadow needs
    its

"Still harping on that?" — 'harping': each gesture, its
   retreat

What's so funny? — serious, a serious breach —
  ": in me" — at least we were both looking at it —
  "When I look out the window, . . . " — "there were
  / farmers out working in the snow." — " . . . I see
  looking; when I look at you,
I see seeing." — both seeing it

1) Rainer Maria Rilke, "Requiem für Eine Freundin"; statement
from a Koan workshop; James McMichael, "Four Good Things";
statement, continued   2) statement, continued

ROUND

Karesansui, Ryoan-ji

gravity — practice — "granite sand, grey" — a monk
    has circled each stone or stone
grouping to rake — like

1) John Berryman, "Dream Song 73: *Karesansui, Ryoan-ji*"

SAVE

"In order to attract the spirits and thus to participate
   in their immortality, [Emperor Wu-ti] is reported
   to have named rocky islands in a large pond or lake
   Islands of Immortality or even to have created such
   islands." — "'He says he wants in his old age to be
   surrounded by the work of his hands.'" — "'Am I
   addressing the White Queen?'
'Well, yes, if you call that a-dressing,' the Queen
   said. 'It isn't *my* notion of the thing, at all.'" — D.
   replied: "You have a strange way of putting things."

1) *Re* Emperor Wu-ti (141–87 B.C.), Irmtraud Schaarschmidt-
Richter and Osamu Mori, *Japanese Gardens*, introduction; Chaim
Potok, *My Name Is Asher Lev*, chapter 8; Lewis Carroll, *Through the
Looking-Glass*, chapter 5 2) Carroll, continued; private conversation
(artist's collection)

SAVING

this small corner of planning — decor — though —
    "little soap // little / soap" — disaster photograph:
a doorframe left standing — just so — *personal void*
    space — " — " — (for "Man be my metaphor"?)
    "Let this be my epitaph."

1) Brenda Hillman, "Cascadia"   2) *personal void space*: area
protected from falling objects during an earthquake (under a table,
for example); Dylan Thomas, "If I were tickled by the rub of love";
source undetermined

"Absorbing the Blow," the martial arts exercise lately
    recommended, an outward spiraling wingspan
    gesture, arching, transported — California — *woo-*
    woo (adjective: from a strain of the Twilight Zone
    theme song?) — Crucifixion/The Passion — 'cross-
    cultural' — Little Joe,
shot in the back in one episode of Bonanza,
    suddenness, enactment, his recoil, *gut-wrenching*: an
    awakening of compassion? (teen) (mine) (remedial?)
    sadistic? sexual? — "and curiouser" — upbringing
    — the Self — loose bouquet

2) Lewis Carroll, *Alice in Wonderland,* chapter 1

would drive her for hours through neighborhoods to
    allay her panic — "(or pay for him / what he owes
    — " — at least there's . . .
[what?] — stripped — Charon — "at the Bone – "
    — "'Can you take care of it now?' 'If not, there's no
    place to avoid.'"

1) Stéphane Mallarmé, *A Tomb for Anatole* (fragment 194) 2) Emily
Dickinson, "[A Narrow Fellow in the Grass]"; Thomas Cleary, *Book
of Serenity*, commentary to "Case (Koan) 87: Sushan's 'Existence
and Nonexistence'"

"Chan Master Guangren of Sushan in Fukien called
    on Dongshan and asked, 'Please teach me the word
    that doesn't yet exist.' Dongshan said, 'When you
    don't consent, no one agrees.' Sushan said, 'Should
    one take care of it?' Dongshan said, 'Can you take
    care of it now?' Sushan said, 'If not, there's no place
    to avoid.'" — a continuum from eye to horizon,
including the eye ("that for me the space is one unity
    from the horizon to the interior of my work room")
    — "the whole of an afternoon" — "'No one
    admitted to the privilege of hearing you, can think
    anything wanting.'"

1) Thomas Cleary, *Book of Serenity*, commentary to "Case (Koan)
87: Sushan's 'Existence and Nonexistence'"; Henri Matisse,
paraphrased from memory.   2) Henri Matisse, 1942 radio interview
in Jack Flam, *Matisse on Art*; Robert Hass, "Santa Barbara Road";
Jane Austen, *Pride and Prejudice*, chapter 31 (Darcy to Elizabeth
Bennett)

"[Fashion] couples the living body to the inorganic
    world. To the living, it defends the rights of the
    corpse." — persistent, my turning away setting
    down a glass, It was murder (as though it were
    murder,
seeing 'us' make that sound) — hefted the gift, held it
    to his ear and shook it — who caroled beautifully;
    but on family walks, her tuneless, bouncy (self-
    conscious?) humming — "'It's only a rattle,'" —
    "'It's only a shadow.' 'Yes, but it's all mine!'"

1) Walter Benjamin, "Paris, Capital of the Nineteenth Century"
(Exposé of 1935)   2) Lewis Carroll, *Through the Looking-Glass*,
chapter 4; *Peter Pan* (musical), after the play by James M. Barrie

TO

would he take my photo: "Before" — up a path to
    the abbot's quarters — by train to Giverny —
    Auschwitz — site . . . 'attraction' —
preserved the ticket — the very shoes

TOWARD

obstruction and its opposite — *is* — the view

"One second there had been nothing"

"and began shifting the bases in and out of various other pairing
combinations. Suddenly I became aware that an adenine-
thymine pair held together by two hydrogen bonds was
identical in shape to a guanine-cytosine pair held together by
at least two hydrogen bonds." — "As we were droning across
Nebraska on the third day, something suddenly happened.
For two weeks I had not thought about physics, and now
it came bursting into my consciousness like an explosion.
Feynman's pictures and Schwinger's equations began sorting
themselves out in my head" — "I became absorbed in
threading my way through the labyrinth of that third act, and
with a shock of recognition I thought I saw clearly where we
had gone wrong, and then, in a sudden flash of improvisation,
exactly the right way to resolve it. I let the swing come to a
full stop and sat there transfixed by the rightness of the idea"
— "I saw it then, quite suddenly, and knew what I would do.
One second there had been nothing,
and then there was the idea."

Epigraph) Chaim Potok, *My Name Is Asher Lev*, chapter 9   1) James D. Watson,
. *The Double Helix*, chapter 26; Freeman Dyson, *Disturbing the Universe*, chapter
6; Moss Hart, *Act One*, part two; Potok   2) Potok, continued

UNDER

"'Now, I daresay you noticed, the last time you picked
    me up, that I was looking rather thoughtful?'
'You *were* a little grave,' said Alice."

1, 2) Lewis Carroll, *Through the Looking-Glass*, chapter 8

or the insights — whether it's the errors almost covered
    over or the efforts — "view of", see: Matisse. *View*
    of Notre-Dame — "to be contemplated, like a
    painting, from a number of fixed vantage points" —
    the errors
almost covered over or the structure or the effort

1) Henri Matisse, Spring 1914: oil on canvas, 147.3 x 94.3 cm.; Günter
Nitschke, *Japanese Gardens*

UNLIKE

a tree of a kind of tree I like — en route — "gave
pleasure" — among sidewalk trees variously
chosen and planted: the weeping [what?] — *What's
your poison?* — position on — "Some say . . . but I
say"

1) Brenda Hillman, "Cascadia"   2) Sappho, "To an army wife, in
Sardis"

UNTIL

a death much like mine? imagined — "—local—" —
    "Black out; Heaven blazing into the head" — "or
    Ought" — *The sudden Reapportionment – / Of Sight*
    — (of dread,
of exemption) — O survivor

1) "Vocabulary Sentences"; W. B. Yeats, "Lapis Lazuli"; Emily
Dickinson, "[After great pain, a formal feeling comes –]"

UNTO

> "an ancient pond—
>   frog jumps in"

effect — "& how does the (((((((((do it" —))))))
)) — 'aural' — as I love you: for it, because of
the ripples? — "each arrangement in its halo . . . of
   raked" — the ripples because

Epigraph) Matsuo Bashō   1) Brenda Hillman, "Doppler Effect in
Diagram Three"   2) "For"

if there *is* a basic good, or good mood — "considering"
    — access: "supplied all of engines," "at the root of
    listening," along the Eightfold Path, "by strong,
    persistent and determined action," "Might I but
    moor – Tonight – / In Thee!", "only by the sound
    / Of a stream flowing"? — "for in a quarter of an
    hour's time there grew up all round about the park
    such a vast number of trees, great and small, bushes
    and brambles, twining one within another" —
    complicated
or wrecked: even the weather! — and heading . . . —
    "when all the great trees, the bushes, and brambles
    gave way of themselves to let him pass through; he
    walked up to the castle" — "Past the bright lake
    up into the temple" — "Thence issuing, we beheld
    again the stars" — I liked the raked look

1) The Seventy Prepositions, according to Mrs. Lenore Larney;
John Berryman, "Dream Song 73: *Karesansui, Ryoan-ji*"; "Near";
Martin Luther King, Jr., "Letter from Birmingham City Jail";
Emily Dickinson, "[Wild Nights – Wild Nights!]"; Dante Aligheri,
Dante's Inferno, canto 34; Andrew Lang, *The Blue Fairy Book*, "The
Sleeping Beauty of the Wood," 2) "Sleeping Beauty"; Berryman;
Dante, *The Portable Dante*

till light through the — *upon my* — "It is not in
    heaven, that you should say: Who shall go up for
    us to heaven, and bring it to us, that we may hear it
    and do it? . . . But the thing is very near to you, in
    your mouth and in your heart, that you" — I loved,
    suddenly, the tree I was pruning: my
ward, my victim, my collaborator

1) Deuteronomy 30:12–14

WITH

facing/faced with — the stations: the lessons —
    "What's the rest of it?" — "To perceive the aura
    of an object we look at means to invest it with the
    ability to look at us in return." — inched,
sitting, the length of the viewing platform, showing
    the [garden] *karesansui* each 'aspect'

1) Thomas Cleary, *Book of Serenity*, "Case [Koan] 52: Caoshan's
'Reality Body'"; Walter Benjamin, "On Some Motifs of Baudelaire"

if I said heaven was . . . above, across . . . along . . . ,
    or *was*, the — O it is there, [. . .] the loop
    [. . .] *regarding* and — synapse [. . .] what
    is held — "occurs —
is located" — (given safety) — "is very near . . . you"

1) "In" 2) "In", continued; Deuteronomy 30:12–14

"The way the drowned leave their names above water."

RYOAN-JI

framed, yet — dry, yet — the gravel, its
rakedness — "how big it is!" — reminiscent, yet

Epigraph) Laura Mullen, "Sestina in Which My Grandmother Is
Going Deaf"   2) John Berryman, "Dream Song 73: *Karesansui,
Ryoan-ji*"

WITHOUT

shock of — ritual of entry — "Formality gave
    pleasure" — bequeathed — from the viewing
    platform,
stones I knew from their photographs! —
    unforeseeable: between

1) Brenda Hillman, "Cascadia"

KARESANSUI SOURCE TEXTS

Adams, Sarah Flower. "Nearer, My God, to Thee" (1841).

Austen, Jane. *Pride and Prejudice*. Oxford: Oxford
    University Press, 1999.

Barrie, James M. *Peter Pan*. See "Other Media," below.

Bashō, Matsuo. *Haiku: Volume VI, Autumn-Winter*. Edited
    by R. H. Blythe. Translation adapted by Carol Snow.
    Tokyo: Hokuseido Press, 1952. "Winter seclusion"

————. In *One Hundred Frogs: From Renga to Haiku to
    English*. Edited by Hiroaki Sato. Translation adapted
    by Carol Snow. New York: John Weatherhill, 1983. "an
    ancient pond"

Beckett, Samuel. *The Unnamable*. New York: Grove Press,
    1958.

Benjamin, Walter. *The Arcades Project*. Translated by
    Howard Eiland and Kevin McLaughin. Cambridge,
    MA: The Belknap Press of Harvard University Press,
    1999. "A [Arcades, Magasins de Noveautiés, Sales
    Clerks]"

————. *Illuminations*. Translated by Harry Zohn. New
    York: Harcourt, Brace & World, 1968. Reprint, New
    York: Schocken Books, 1969. "On Some Motifs of
    Baudelaire"

Berryman, John. *The Dream Songs*. New York: Farrar,
    Straus and Giroux, 1959. "Dream Song 1";"Dream Song
    73: *Karesansui, Ryoan-ji*"

————. *Delusions, Etc.* New York: Farrar, Straus and
    Giroux, 1972. "Henry's Confession"

Bishop, Elizabeth. *The Complete Poems 1927–1979*. New York: Farrar, Straus and Giroux, 1983. "Five Flights Up"

Carroll, Lewis. *Alice's Adventures in Wonderland and Through the Looking-Glass*. New York: Penguin Putnam, 1998.

Chast, Roz. See "Artworks," below.

Cleary, Thomas. *Book of Serenity*. Translated by Thomas Cleary. Hudson, New York: Lindesfarne Press, 1990.

Clover, Joshua. *Madonna anno domini*. Baton Rouge: Louisiana State University Press, 1997. "Union pacific"
———. *The Totality for Kids*. Berkeley and Los Angeles: University of California Press, 2006. "Chreia"

Dante Alighieri. *Dante's Inferno*. Translated by John D. Sinclair. New York: Oxford University Press, 1961.
———. *The Portable Dante*. Edited by Paolo Milano. New York: The Viking Press, 1947. Reprint, New York: Penguin Books, 1977. "The Divine Comedy: Inferno," translated by Laurence Binyon

Deuteronomy 30:12–14. Translated possibly by Chaim Potok. See Potok, *My Name Is Asher Lev.*

Dickinson, Emily. *The Poems of Emily Dickinson*. Edited by Thomas H. Johnson. Cambridge, MA: The Belknap Press of Harvard University Press, 1983. "[After great pain, a formal feeling comes –]"; "[The Brain – is wider than the Sky –]"; "[A Narrow Fellow in the Grass]"; "[There's a certain Slant of light]"; "[Wild Nights – Wild Nights!]"

Duncan, Robert. *Selected Poems*. New York: New Directions, 1993. "'My Mother Would Be a Falconress'"

Dyson, Freeman. *Disturbing the Universe*. New York: Harper and Row, 1979.

Flam, Jack. *Matisse and Picasso: The Story of Their Rivalry and Friendship*. Cambridge, MA: Westview Press, 2004.

————, ed. *Matisse on Art*. Berkeley and Los Angeles: University of California Press, 1995. "Portraits, 1954"; "Radio Interview, 1942"

Fukuda, Kazuhiko. *Japanese Stone Gardens: How to Make and Enjoy Them*. Rutland, VT: C. E. Tuttle Co., 1970.

Glazer, Michele. *It Is Hard to Look at What We Came to Think We Came to See*. Pittsburgh, PA: University of Pittsburgh Press, 1997. "And Sand Dollars"

Gleick, James. *Genius: The Life and Science of Richard Feynman*. New York: Pantheon Books, 1992.

Graham, Jorie. *The End of Beauty*. New York: Ecco Press, 1987. "To the Reader"

Greenberg, Joanna (as Hannah Green). *I Never Promised You a Rose Garden*. New York: Holt, Reinhart and Winston, 1964.

Hart, Moss. *Act One: An Autobiography*. New York: Random House, 1959. Reprint, New York: St. Martin's Press, 1989.

Hass, Robert. *Human Wishes*. New York: Ecco Press, 1989. "Interrupted Meditation"; "Santa Barbara Road"

————. *Praise*. New York: Ecco Press, 1974. "Not Going to New York: A Letter"

Heidegger, Martin. *On the Way to Language*. Translated by Peter D. Hertz. New York: Harper and Row, 1971. "A Dialog on Language"

Herrigel, Eugen. *Zen in the Art of Archery*. Translated by R. F. C. Hull. New York: Pantheon Books, 1953. Reprint, New York: Vintage Books, 1971.

Hillman, Brenda. *Cascadia*. Middletown, CT: Wesleyan University Press, 2001. "Cascadia"

————. *Loose Sugar*. Hanover, CT: Wesleyan University Press, 1997. "Time Problem"

———. *Pieces of Air in the Epic.* Middletown, CT:
    Wesleyan University Press, 2005. *"Doppler Effect in
    Diagram Three"*

Huffington, Arianna Stassinopoulos. *Picasso: Creator and
    Destroyer.* New York: Simon & Schuster, 1988.

Issa, Kobayashi. *The Essential Haiku: Versions of Basho,
    Buson, and Issa.* Translated by Robert Hass. Hopewell,
    NJ: Ecco Press, 1994. "[The world of dew]"

King, Jr., Martin Luther. *A Testament of Hope: The Essential
    Writing and Speeches of Martin Luther King, Jr.* Edited
    by James M. Washington. New York: HarperOne,
    1990. "Letter from Birmingham City Jail"

Lang, Andrew. *The Blue Fairy Book.* Edited by Andrew
    Lang. New York: Dover Publications, 1965. "The
    Sleeping Beauty of the Wood"

Larson, Gary. See "Artworks," below.

Mallarmé, Stéphane. *A Tomb for Anatole.* Translated by
    Paul Auster. San Francisco: North Point Press, 1983.

McMichael, James. *The World at Large: New and Selected
    Poems, 1971–1996.* Chicago: University of Chicago Press,
    1996. "Four Good Things"

Mullen, Laura. *The Surface.* Urbana: University of Illinois
    Press, 1991. "Sestina in Which My Grandmother Is
    Going Deaf"

Nitschke, Günter. *Japanese Gardens: Right Angle and
    Natural Form.* Translated by Karen Williams. Cologne:
    Benedict Taschen, 1993.

O'Hara, Frank. *The Collected Poems of Frank O'Hara.*
    Edited by Donald Allen. Berkeley: University of
    California Press, 1995. "The Day Lady Died"

Oppen, George. *New Collected Poems.* New York: New
    Directions, 2002. "Of Being Numerous"

Park, Clara Claiborne. *Exiting Nirvana: A Daughter's Life with Autism*. New York: Little, Brown and Company, 2001.

Pessoa, Fernando (as Alvaro de Campos). *Pessoa & Co.* Translated by Richard Zenith. New York: Grove Press, 1998. "Impassively"

———. In *Pen America 5: Silences*. Translated by Richard Zenith. New York: Pen American Journal, 2004. "Peristyle," translated and quoted by Richard Zenith in "Pessoa's Disquiet"

Potok, Chaim. *My Name Is Asher Lev*. New York: Knopf, 1972.

Rilke, Rainer Maria. *The Selected Poetry of Rainer Maria Rilke*. Edited and translated by Stephen Mitchell. New York: Random House, 1982. "Requieum für Eine Freundin"

Sappho. *Sappho: A New Translation*. Translated by Mary Barnard. Berkeley: University of California Press, 1958. "To an army wife, in Sardis"

Schaarschmidt-Richter, Irmtraud and Osamu Mori. *Japanese Gardens*. Translated by Janet Seligman. New York: Morrow, 1979.

Seung Sahn. *The Compass of Zen* (Boston and London: Shambhala, 1997).

Shakespeare, William. *William Shakespeare: The Complete Works*. New York: Penguin, 2002. *Hamlet*, *Julius Caesar*, *Macbeth*

Slawson, David A. *Secret Teachings in the Art of Japanese Gardens*. New York: Kodansha International, 1987.

Snow, Carol. *Artist and Model*. New York: Atlantic Monthly Press, 1990. "Bridge"; "Living in Venice"; "Positions of the Body"

————. *For.* Berkeley: University of California Press, 2000. "By the Pond"; "For"; "Bowl"

————. *The Seventy Prepositions.* Berkeley: University of California Press, 2004. "Bit"; "Conversion ('Spin')"; "Some Not"; "Trace"; "Vocabulary Sentences"

Som, Indigo. Artist's statement from the catalog to "Unbound and Under Covers," Berkeley Art Center, 2003. Curated by Jamie Robles.

Stein, Gertrude. *Selected Writings of Gertrude Stein.* Edited by Carl Van Vecten. New York: Random House, 1962. "The Gradual Making of The Making of Americans"

————. *How to Write.* New York: Dover Publications, 1975. "Sentences"

Stockton, Frank Richard. *The Best Short Stories of Frank R. Stockton.* New York: Scribner's, 1957.

Thomas, Dylan. *The Collected Poems of Dylan Thomas 1934–1952.* New York: New Directions, 1971. "And Death Shall Have No Dominion;" "If I were tickled by the rub of love"

Tranströmer, Tomas. *Selected Poems 1954–1986.* Edited by Robert Hass. New York: Ecco Press, 1987. "Streets of Shanghai", translated by Samuel Charters

Watson, James D. *The Double Helix: A Personal Account of the Discovery of the Structure of DNA.* New York: Atheneum, 1968.

Wordsworth, William. *The Norton Anthology of Poetry.* Edited by Arthur M. Eastman et al. New York: W. W. Norton and Company, 1970. "A Slumber Did My Spirit Seal"

Yeats, William Butler. *Selected Poems and Two Plays of William Butler Yeats.* Edited and with an introduction by M. L. Rosenthal. New York: Macmillan, 1962. Reprint, New York: Collier, 1966.

Chast, Roz. *Theories of Everything: Selected, Collected, Health-Inspected Cartoons by Roz Chast 1978–2006.* New York: Bloomsbury Publishing, 2006. "The Lady, or the Tiger, or the Closet?"

Larson, Gary. *The Complete Far Side, Volume 1.* Kansas City, MO: Andrews McMeel, 2003. "I just love these things . . . " (1980)

Matisse, Henri. *La leçon de piano (The Piano Lesson).* Summer 1916. Oil on canvas, 245.1 x 212.7 cm. The Museum of Modern Art, New York. Mrs. Simon Guggenheim Fund, formerly collections of Paul Guillaume; Walter P. Chrysler, Jr.

Matisse, Henri. *Une vue de Notre-Dame (View of Notre Dame).* Spring 1914. Oil on canvas, 147.3 x 94.3 cm. The Museum of Modern Art, New York. Note: there is another, more representational, "View of Notre-Dame" from this same period.

Picasso, Pablo. *Guitar, Sheet Music and Glass ("La Bataille s'est engagé[e]").* Late 1912. Pasted papers, goache, and charcoal on paper, 48 x 36.5 cm. Bequest of Marion Koogler McKay, McNay Art Museum, San Antonio, Texas.

OTHER MEDIA

Beyond the Fringe '64, Volume 2. Original Broadway cast recording. New York: Capitol Records, 1964. Alan Bennett, Peter Cook, Jonathan Miller, and Dudley Moore. "The Great Train Robbery"

James Taylor: Best Live. Music and lyrics by James Taylor.
New York: Sony, 1994. "Fire and Rain"

Peter Pan. Original Broadway cast recording. New York:
R. C. A. Victor, 1954. Music and lyrics by Jule Styne,
Betty Comden, Adolph Green, Mark Charlap, Carolyn
Leigh, and Trude Rittman, with incidental music by
Trude Rittman and Elmer Bernstein. Based on the play
by Sir James M. Barrie. Spoken introduction to "I've
Gotta Crow"

Horse Feathers. Motion picture. Bert Kalmar, S. J.
Perelman et al; Adolph Zukor presents, directed
by Norman Z. McLeod. Paramount Pictures, 1932.
Professor Wagstaff (Groucho Marx) lectures on the
circulatory system: "The blood rushes from the head
down to the feet, gets a look at those feet, and rushes
back to the head again."

DEDICATIONS

"Beside" — for James Kapp, in memoriam
"Between" — for David Matchett
"Despite" — for Joan Landsberg
"Respecting" — for Tenshin Reb Anderson
"Through" — for Adrienne
"To" — for Elizabeth Abel
"Up" — for Laura Mullen

ACKNOWLEDGMENTS

Sincere thanks to the editors of the following publications, in which versions of some of these poems first appeared: *Carnet de Route, Denver Quarterly, Electronic Poetry Review, Eleven Eleven, English Language Notes, Volt, Xantippe*. Versions of some of the *karesansui* poems were previously published in *The Seventy Prepositions*, University of California Press; many thanks to the Regents, editors and staff.

Thank you, David Matchett, every day. Warm appreciation to Patricia Dientsfrey, Susan Kolodny, and Denise Newman for meaningful attention and advice; to Gary Hauser for the delight of "a hundred studies"; and to Bill and Judy Matchett for the first pilgrimage. For above and beyond—for this collection in particular—my heartfelt gratitude to Laura Mullen.

Carol Snow is the author of *Artist and Model* (selected by Robert Hass for the National Poetry Series and winner of the Poetry Center Book Award), *For*, and *The Seventy Prepositions* (both published by the University of California Press). She has received the Joseph Henry Jackson Award in Literature, a Poetry Fund grant, a Pushcart Prize, and a National Endowment for the Arts Fellowship. She lives and works in her native San Francisco.